# Grammar and Punctuation

## Book 3

Louis Fidge

# Using this book

*This book will help you to understand grammar and punctuation, and improve your writing. You will learn how sentences are structured and formed, how words work together and the rules of our language. Punctuation goes hand in hand with grammar – punctuation marks make writing easier to understand.*

## What's in a unit

Each unit is set out in the same way as the example here. There are also Progress Units to help you check how well you are doing.

**Unit heading**
This tells you what you will be learning about

**The rule**
This explains the rule and gives an example

**Making sure**
Activities to practise and develop your understanding

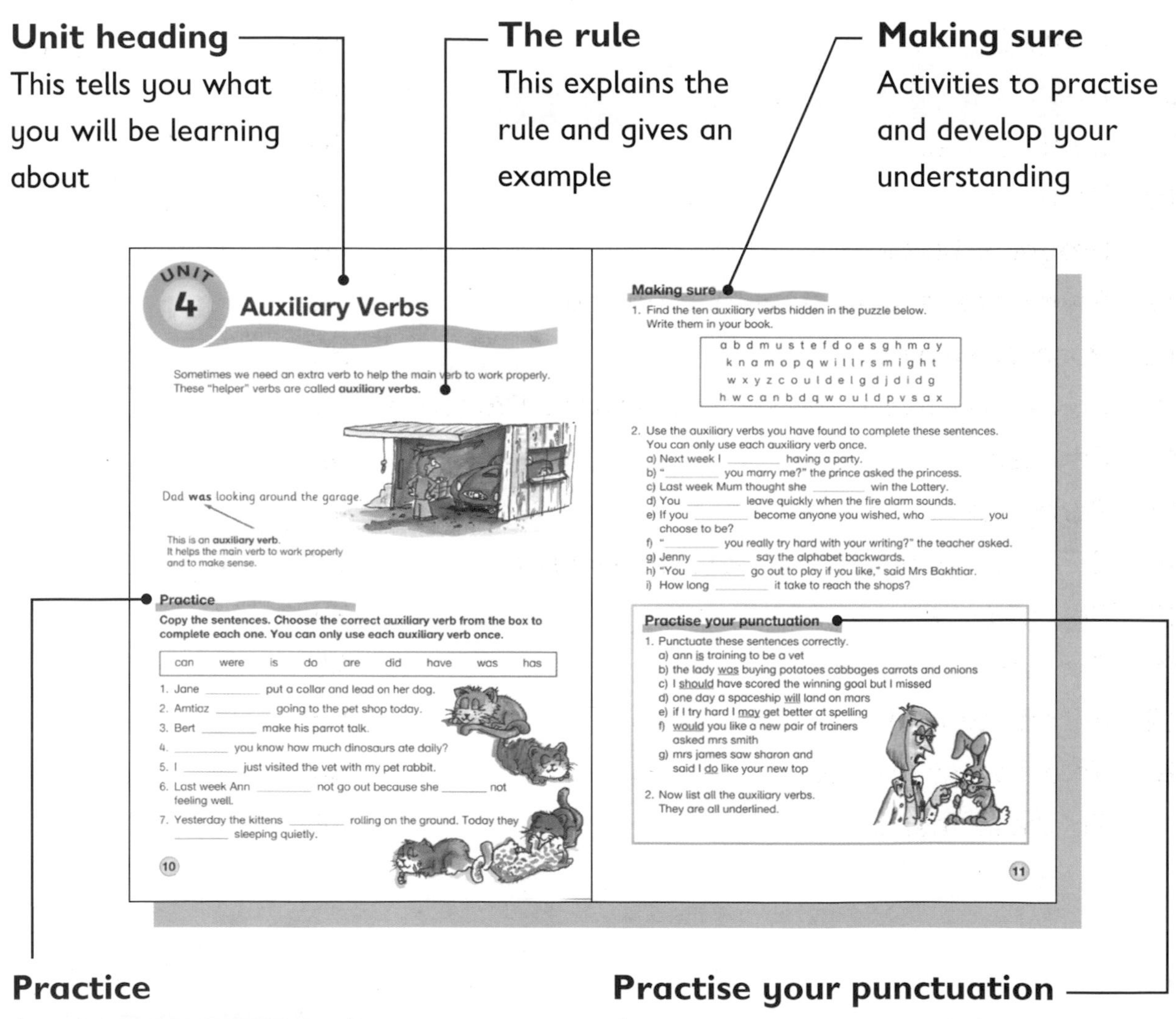

UNIT 4 **Auxiliary Verbs**

Sometimes we need an extra verb to help the main verb to work properly.
These "helper" verbs are called **auxiliary verbs.**

Dad **was** looking around the garage.

This is an **auxiliary verb**.
It helps the main verb to work properly and to make sense.

**Practice**

**Copy the sentences. Choose the correct auxiliary verb from the box to complete each one. You can only use each auxiliary verb once.**

| can | were | is | do | are | did | have | was | has |
|---|---|---|---|---|---|---|---|---|

1. Jane ________ put a collar and lead on her dog.
2. Amtiaz ________ going to the pet shop today.
3. Bert ________ make his parrot talk.
4. ________ you know how much dinosaurs ate daily?
5. I ________ just visited the vet with my pet rabbit.
6. Last week Ann ________ not go out because she ________ not feeling well.
7. Yesterday the kittens ________ rolling on the ground. Today they ________ sleeping quietly.

10

**Making sure**

1. Find the ten auxiliary verbs hidden in the puzzle below.
   Write them in your book.

| a b d m u s t e f d o e s g h m a y |
|---|
| k n a m o p q w i l l r s m i g h t |
| w x y z c o u l d e l g d j d i d g |
| h w c a n b d q w o u l d p v s a x |

2. Use the auxiliary verbs you have found to complete these sentences.
   You can only use each auxiliary verb once.
   a) Next week I ________ having a party.
   b) "________ you marry me?" the prince asked the princess.
   c) Last week Mum thought she ________ win the Lottery.
   d) You ________ leave quickly when the fire alarm sounds.
   e) If you ________ become anyone you wished, who ________ you choose to be?
   f) "________ you really try hard with your writing?" the teacher asked.
   g) Jenny ________ say the alphabet backwards.
   h) "You ________ go out to play if you like," said Mrs Bakhtiar.
   i) How long ________ it take to reach the shops?

**Practise your punctuation**

1. Punctuate these sentences correctly.
   a) ann is training to be a vet
   b) the lady was buying potatoes cabbages carrots and onions
   c) I should have scored the winning goal but I missed
   d) one day a spaceship will land on mars
   e) if I try hard I may get better at spelling
   f) would you like a new pair of trainers asked mrs smith
   g) mrs james saw sharon and said I do like your new top
2. Now list all the auxiliary verbs.
   They are all underlined.

11

**Practice**
Activities to practise and check your understanding

**Practise your punctuation**
Activities to practise and check your punctuation

# Contents

UNIT 1

# Parts of Speech
## (nouns, adjectives, verbs and adverbs)

**Grammar** is the study of the way in which we use words to make **sentences**.
Words may be divided into groups called **parts of speech**.
Four important **parts of speech** are:
**nouns**, **adjectives**, **verbs** and **adverbs**.

This is an **adjective**.
It **describes** the fish.

The **spotted fish swam slowly**.

This is an **adverb**.
It tells us more about the **verb**.

This is a **noun**.
A **noun** is a **naming word**.

This is a **verb**.
A **verb** is a word that describes **actions**.

## Practice

1. Copy the sentences. Choose a noun and an adjective to complete each one.

| *Nouns* | | |
|---|---|---|
| wings | water | frog |

| *Adjectives* | | |
|---|---|---|
| fat | silver | frightened |

a) I could see the ________ fish in the ________.
b) The ________ ________ hopped into the pond.
c) The small bird flapped its ________ because it was ________.

2. Copy the sentences. Choose a verb and an adverb to complete each one.

| *Verbs* | | |
|---|---|---|
| served | ate | hooted |

| *Adverbs* | | |
|---|---|---|
| angrily | quickly | gently |

a) The driver ________ his horn and shook his fist ________.
b) Megan ________ her sandwiches ________ and drank her drink thirstily.
c) The waiter put the tray down ________ when he ________ our drinks.

## Making sure

**Copy and complete these charts.**

1.

| *Noun* | *Adjective* |
|---|---|
| anger | angry |
| | beautiful |
| comfort | |
| | dangerous |
| expense | |
| | famous |
| nation | |
| | historic |
| | woollen |
| fury | |

2.

| *Verb* | *Noun* |
|---|---|
| act | action |
| arrive | |
| | behaviour |
| compare | |
| | delivery |
| encourage | |
| | entrance |
| | hatred |
| marry | |
| | pressure |

3.

| *Adjective* | *Adverb* |
|---|---|
| clever | cleverly |
| | clearly |
| wide | |
| | roughly |
| able | |
| bad | |
| | carefully |
| lucky | |
| | noisily |
| faithful | |

## Practise your punctuation

1. Punctuation marks make writing easier to understand. Punctuate these sentences correctly.
   a) have you seen my ring Ive lost it ring me up if you find it
   b) tom took the sweet apple but vicky took the sweet
   c) crash the lift broke when I tried to lift the heavy case into it
   d) the archaeologist found a large stone inside the stone vase

2. In each sentence, underline the two words that are the same. One of the words must be a noun. Above each word:
   a) write **a** if it is an adjective
   b) write **n** if it is a noun
   c) write **v** if it is a verb

# UNIT 2 Types of Sentence

There are four different types of sentence:

- **statements**
- **questions**
- **commands**
- **exclamations**

This is a **statement**. A **statement** is a sentence which gives us **information**.

This is a **question**. A **question asks** something. A **question** finishes with a **question mark**.

This is a **command**. A **command** tells someone to **do something**.

This is an **exclamation**. An **exclamation** shows that a person **feels** something strongly. An **exclamation** finishes with an **exclamation mark**.

## Practice

1. Write a statement to answer each question.
   a) What is for lunch today?
   b) What can you see from the window?
   c) Who is your favourite singer?
   d) When did it last rain?
   e) How are you dressed today?
   f) Where is Paris?

2. Make these statements into questions by changing them a little. The first one has been done for you.
   a) Jo often copies Kimberley's work.
      Does Jo often copy Kimberley's work?
   b) Khayyam's book is very messy.
   c) Mrs Saunders shouted at Bethany.
   d) The dragon was long and thin.
   e) Andrea is good at art.
   f) There are no such things as unicorns.

## Making sure

1. These instructions tell you how to make a clay pot.

   a) Write them in the correct order.

   Roll the clay into a round ball.
   Leave your pot to dry.
   Heat the kiln to bake your pot.
   Smooth the outside of your pot.
   Get a lump of moist clay.
   Put your dry pot into a kiln.
   Make a pot shape.

   b) Now underline all the verbs.

2. Look at these exclamations. For each one, write a sentence about the person who could be speaking and what you think is happening.

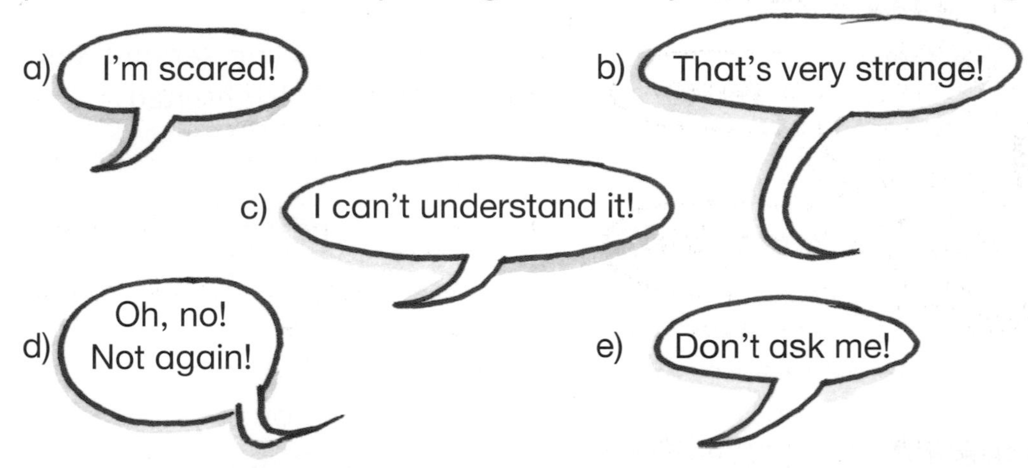


## Practise your punctuation

1. Punctuate these sentences correctly.
   a) how far is it to the houses of parliament
   b) bring me my book pencil ruler and crayons jack
   c) were all going to jamaica for our summer holiday
   d) my house is on fire

2. After each sentence:
   a) write **s** if it is a statement
   b) write **q** if it is a question
   c) write **c** if it is a command
   d) write **e** if it is an exclamation

# UNIT 3 Verb Tenses (past)

**Verbs** written in the **past tense** tell us what happened **some time ago**.

**live** **call** **come** **is**

The rich man **lived** in a mansion. He **called** his servant.

The servant **came** in.

The servant **was** frightened.

Some verbs add **d** or **ed** to make the past tense.

Some verbs change the middle vowel sound to make the past tense.

Some verbs change completely to make the past tense.

## Practice

1. Write the past tense of each of these verbs by changing its middle vowel sound. The first one has been done for you.

| | | |
|---|---|---|
| a) get ⟶ got | b) sit | c) give |
| d) sing | e) fall | f) throw |
| g) hold | h) dig | i) stick |
| j) sink | k) begin | l) ride |
| m) grow | n) blow | o) swim |

2. Write these sentences again. Put the verbs into the past tense.
   a) I hold the baby gently in my arms.
   b) I dig the garden with a fork.
   c) I get hot in the sun.
   d) I sing in the bath.
   e) I sit in the most comfortable chair.
   f) I ride my bike in the park.
   g) I swim in the sea.
   h) I begin my meal with a bowl of soup.

## Making sure

1. Match each verb in Box A with its past tense in Box B. The first one has been done for you.

| *Box A* | is are think buy say keep feel sleep leave go do kneel catch have wear eat |
|---|---|

| *Box B* | thought kept left went had ate was did were slept said knelt wore bought caught felt |
|---|---|

is ⟶ was

2. Copy the sentences. Fill each one with a suitable verb from Box B.
   a) Last week my mum __________ me a new school uniform.
   b) The teacher __________, "I __________ that __________ very silly!"
   c) We __________ working very hard.
   d) When I __________ in the tent, I __________ a torch under my pillow.
   e) Yesterday I __________ my bag at school by mistake.
   f) A short while ago I __________ a very bad cold.
   g) I __________ up to my bedroom for a bit of peace.

## Practise your punctuation

1. Punctuate these sentences correctly.
   a) harry sits on the settee and turns on the television
   b) the teacher asked who threw that book
   c) the train to luton stops at every station
   d) I creep up the stairs quietly and frighten my brother
   e) beth and alice rode their bikes home on saturday
   f) stop come here at once
   g) yesterday we saw lots of interesting things on our trip
   h) at the shop amy bought some apples pears bananas and grapes

2. Underline the verb or verbs in each sentence.

3. At the end of each sentence:
   a) write **pr** if the verb(s) are in the present tense
   b) write **pa** if the verb(s) are in the past tense

UNIT 4

# Auxiliary Verbs

Sometimes we need an extra verb to help the main verb to work properly. These "helper" verbs are called **auxiliary verbs**.

Dad **was** looking around the garage.

This is an **auxiliary verb**.
It helps the main verb to work properly and to make sense.

## Practice

**Copy the sentences. Choose the correct auxiliary verb from the box to complete each one. You can only use each auxiliary verb once.**

| can | were | is | do | are | did | have | was | has |
|---|---|---|---|---|---|---|---|---|

1. Jane _________ put a collar and lead on her dog.
2. Amtiaz _________ going to the pet shop today.
3. Bert _________ make his parrot talk.
4. _________ you know how much dinosaurs ate daily?
5. I _________ just visited the vet with my pet rabbit.
6. Last week Ann _________ not go out because she _________ not feeling well.
7. Yesterday the kittens _________ rolling on the ground. Today they _________ sleeping quietly.

## Making sure

1. Find the ten auxiliary verbs hidden in the puzzle below.
   Write them in your book.

| a b d m u s t e f d o e s g h m a y |
|---|
| k n a m o p q w i l l r s m i g h t |
| w x y z c o u l d e l g d j d i d g |
| h w c a n b d q w o u l d p v s a x |

2. Use the auxiliary verbs you have found to complete these sentences.
   You can only use each auxiliary verb once.
   a) Next week I __________ having a party.
   b) "__________ you marry me?" the prince asked the princess.
   c) Last week Mum thought she __________ win the Lottery.
   d) You __________ leave quickly when the fire alarm sounds.
   e) If you __________ become anyone you wished, who __________ you choose to be?
   f) "__________ you really try hard with your writing?" the teacher asked.
   g) Jenny __________ say the alphabet backwards.
   h) "You __________ go out to play if you like," said Mrs Bakhtiar.
   i) How long __________ it take to reach the shops?

## Practise your punctuation

1. Punctuate these sentences correctly.
   a) ann is training to be a vet
   b) the lady was buying potatoes cabbages carrots and onions
   c) I should have scored the winning goal but I missed
   d) one day a spaceship will land on mars
   e) if I try hard I may get better at spelling
   f) would you like a new pair of trainers asked mrs smith
   g) mrs james saw sharon and said I do like your new top

2. Now list all the auxiliary verbs.
   They are all underlined.

# UNIT 5 Adjectives (comparatives and superlatives)

An **adjective** is a **describing** word.
When we **compare two nouns** we use a **comparative adjective**.
When we **compare three or more nouns** we use a **superlative adjective**.

small

small**er**

When the adjective is short, the **comparative** form usually ends in **er**.

small**est**

When the adjective is short, the **superlative** form usually ends in **est**.

powerful

**more** powerful

**most** powerful

When the adjective is long, it sounds strange to add **er** or **est**.
We use the word **more** to make the **comparative** form.
We use the word **most** to make the **superlative** form.

## Practice

**Copy and complete this chart.**

| *Adjective* | *Comparative adjective* | *Superlative adjective* |
|---|---|---|
| 1. wise | wiser | wisest |
| 2. big | | |
| 3. happy | | |
| 4. beautiful | | |
| 5. comfortable | | |
| 6. dangerous | | |

## Making sure

**A few adjectives do not follow any of the rules on page 12. You just have to learn these.**

| *Adjective* | *Comparative adjective* | *Superlative adjective* |
|---|---|---|
| good | better | best |
| bad | worse | worst |
| little | less | least |
| many | more | most |

**Write the comparative and superlative forms of these adjectives. The first one has been done for you.**

1. bright ⟶ brighter ⟶ brightest

2. bad
3. delightful
4. funny
5. terrible
6. good
7. pretty
8. little
9. unpleasant
10. many
11. honest
12. wet
13. foolish
14. natural
15. musical

## Practise your punctuation

1. Punctuate these sentences correctly.
   a) mrs turner is rich but mr barnes is richer mrs yates is the richest
   b) sheep are noisy but cows are noisier cockerels are by far the noisiest of the farm animals
   c) one slice of pizza is good two slices of pizza are better the whole pizza is best
   d) the smith family is very quarrelsome but the brown family is even more quarrelsome the parker family is the most quarrelsome family in our street
   e) two meals a day is bad one meal a day is worse no meals a day is worst of all

2. In the sentences you have written:
   a) underline the comparative adjectives
   b) circle the superlative adjectives

UNIT 6

# Adverbs (of manner, time and place)

An **adverb** is a word which gives **more meaning** to a **verb**.

The magician waved his wand **mysteriously**.

An **adverb of manner** tells us **how** something happened.

**Next**, a puff of smoke appeared.

An **adverb of time** tells us **when** something happened.

He pulled **out** a rabbit.

An **adverb of place** tells us **where** something happened.

## Practice

1. Copy the sentences. Underline the verb in each one.
   a) The snow fell thickly.
   b) Listen carefully.
   c) It rained heavily on the tent.
   d) I hit the table angrily with my fist.
   e) Sara wrote the letter neatly.
   f) A tear slowly trickled down my cheek.
   g) The cat stretched lazily.
   h) The dog ate his dinner greedily.
   i) Tom threw the ball accurately.
   j) Slowly the giant stretched his arms and legs.

2. Now circle the adverb of manner in each sentence.

3. Make up some sentences of your own. Include these adverbs of time and place in them.

| *Adverbs of time* | *Adverbs of place* |
|---|---|
| now tomorrow first always after | down everywhere in outside left |

## Making sure

**Draw a chart like this. Write each adverb from the box in the correct column.**

| *Adverbs of manner (how?)* | *Adverbs of time (when?)* | *Adverbs of place (where?)* |
|---|---|---|
| | | |

later quickly gently often yesterday in
suspiciously tidily out inside afterwards now
bravely everywhere sweetly next then here
there deeply up finally always carefully

## Practise your punctuation

1. Punctuate this passage correctly.

   yesterday I saw two birds busily building their nest they flew backwards and forwards up and down and in and out first they found some twigs next they carefully wove them into a nest they tirelessly pulled and tugged it into shape this wasnt all they did finally they carefully lined it with moss soon the female bird will lay her eggs

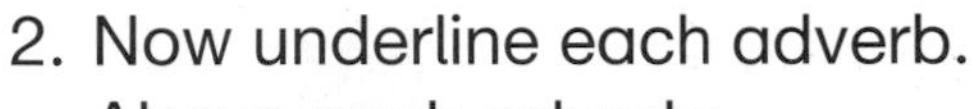

2. Now underline each adverb.
   Above each adverb:
   a) write **m** if it is an adverb of manner
   b) write **t** if it is an adverb of time
   c) write **p** if it is an adverb of place

# UNIT 7 Using Commas

A **comma** is a **punctuation mark**. This is a comma. ,
**Commas** show us where to take a slight **pause**.
**Commas** help us to understand the **meaning** of a sentence.

In the cold, dark, silent depths of the sea, the shark lies in waiting.

The shark, with its black back and white stomach, has a terrible bite.

## Practice

1. Punctuate these phrases with commas.
   a) a nasty mean spiteful man
   b) dirty careless scruffy writing
   c) hot bright sunny days
   d) some cold clear sparkling water
   e) a huge angry lumbering monster
   f) a cool shady leafy forest

2. Rewrite these sentences. Put in a comma where the reader needs to pause.
   a) The Pyramids which are in Egypt are enormous.
   b) Barney who came last was very upset.
   c) Mr Younnas our next-door neighbour is very nice.
   d) However hard she tried Wendy could not catch any fish.
   e) We arrived in Paris the capital of France.
   f) Jane my sister is good at singing.
   g) The River Thames a very long river flows through London.
   h) Visit Australia the land of opportunity.

## Making sure

**Punctuate these sentences correctly. Think carefully about where to put the commas.**

1. dogs don't wear glasses do they
2. what's the matter johnny
3. oh dear the lift is stuck
4. half an hour later sophie came out of the cinema
5. please sir can you help me
6. from monday to friday the shop closes at five o'clock
7. if you turn left you will soon come to the park
8. should I put vinegar on the chips or not yes you should
9. hello mr salim it's very hot isn't it
10. in a cave on the far side of the mountain there lived a dragon
11. louise who was only nine easily won the race
12. st george brave and valiant saved the maiden

## Practise your punctuation

**These sentences don't make sense because some commas and full stops are missing or in the wrong places. Try to rewrite them so that they make more sense.**

1. The king walked and talked half an hour after his head was cut off.
2. The soldier entered on his head, a helmet on each foot, a sandal in his hand. He had his trusty sword.
3. The giant had hairy feet, huge and flat, on his head. He squashed his hat over his shoulder. He carried a club, big and spiky, in his hand. A sword he waved.

UNIT 8

# Nouns
## (singular and plural)

We can write **nouns** in the **singular** or the **plural**.
**Singular** means **just one**. **Plural** means **more than one**.

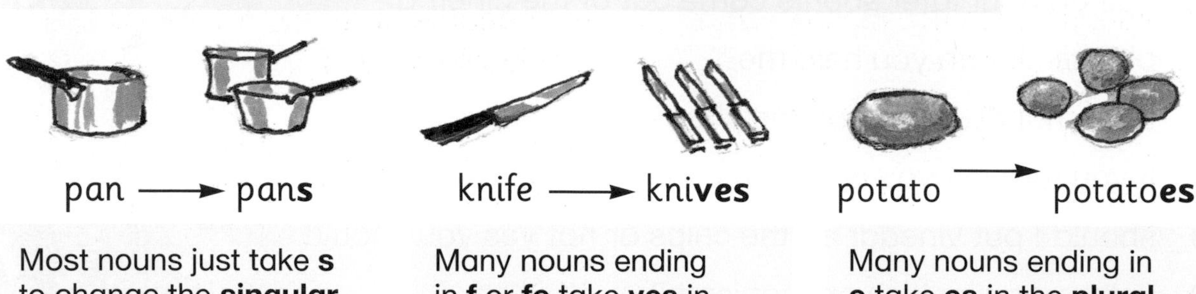

pan ⟶ pan**s**

knife ⟶ kni**ves**

potato ⟶ potato**es**

Most nouns just take **s** to change the **singular** into the **plural** form.

Many nouns ending in **f** or **fe** take **ves** in the **plural**.
Common exceptions are: **chiefs**, **roofs**

Many nouns ending in **o** take **es** in the **plural**.
Common exceptions are: **photos**, **videos**, **pianos**, **hippos**

## Practice

1. Write the plural forms of these nouns.
   a) thief b) dog c) hero d) neighbour e) leaf
   f) wife g) echo h) wolf i) letter j) tomato

2. Write the singular forms of these nouns.
   a) volcanoes b) halves c) lives d) houses e) dingoes
   f) loaves g) steps h) cargoes i) dominoes j) calves

3. Some nouns are not regular. They do not follow any rules.
   Copy these irregular nouns. Match the singular and the plural forms.

| *Singular* | *Plural* |
|---|---|
| woman | children |
| goose | feet |
| foot | women |
| deer | teeth |
| child | deer |
| tooth | geese |

## Making sure

1. Think of a suitable plural noun to complete each phrase.
   The first one has been done for you.

   a) a pack of _wolves_    b) a herd of ________
   c) a team of ________    d) a shoal of ________
   e) a library of ________    f) a swarm of ________
   g) a forest of ________    h) a pile of ________

2 Nouns which are the names of groups of people or things are called collective nouns. Think of a suitable collective noun to complete each phrase.

   a) a ________ of bananas    b) a ________ of ships
   c) a ________ of thieves    d) a ________ of cards
   e) a ________ of singers    f) a ________ of kittens
   g) a ________ of arrows    h) a ________ of clothes

## Practise your punctuation

1. Punctuate these sentences correctly.
   a) this morning the thieves were arrested
   b) the baker said sam put the loaves on the shelves please
   c) are the baked potatoes ready yet
   d) during the night the leaves fell off the trees
   e) mr smith the tomatoes you sold me were rotten

2. Underline the plural nouns.

3. Now write the sentences again. Change the plural nouns into singular nouns. Remember to make the verbs agree with the nouns.

UNIT 9

# Direct Speech

When we write down the exact words someone has spoken, we call this **direct speech**.
We use **inverted commas** to mark the beginning and end of what the person said. These are **inverted commas**. “ ”

Here are two ways of writing this down as **direct speech**.
Notice the use of a **comma** in both sentences.

The old woman said**, “This is for you.”**

**“This is for you,”** the old woman said.

## Practice

**Copy these sentences. Put the inverted commas in the correct places.**

1. Wait here, the teacher said.
2. The boy shouted, Catch the ball.
3. Please let me go, begged the thief.
4. The old lady said, Don’t worry. I won’t hurt you.
5. I’m going to get an ice cream, the small girl squealed excitedly.
6. Cut down that tree, commanded the woodcutter.
7. I’m lost. Which way is it to Ipswich? enquired the motorist.
8. James asked, What time is it?
9. The house is on fire! Get out of here fast! shouted Jenna.
10. I’m hungry. It must be nearly home time, whispered Anna.

## Making sure

**Sometimes the speaker's name comes in the middle of the direct speech. Copy these sentences. Put in the inverted commas.**

1. Help! screamed Emma. I'm drowning!
2. Sit down, said the teacher, and get on with your work.
3. Can I be of assistance? the shopkeeper asked. Is there anything I can show you?
4. Look at this picture! exclaimed Francis. It's really lovely!
5. Quick! Pass the ball! shouted Lee. No one is marking me!
6. I can't come out, explained Indira. I've got too much homework.
7. I dropped my ring somewhere, explained Ann, but I can't seem to find it.
8. I'll meet you in town, Mrs Turner said, outside the supermarket.
9. You're early, said the waiter. Your table is not ready yet.
10. It's no use crying, snapped Nina's mum. You will only make things worse.

## Practise your punctuation

**Write these conversations as sentences. The first one has been done for you.**

1. Samir: I'm bored. What shall we do?
   Emma: Let's go to the park.

   "I'm bored," said Samir. " What shall we do?"
   "Let's go to the park," said Emma.

2. Holly: I like these jeans best. Can I have them?
   Mum: No, you can't! I'm not spending all that money on a pair of jeans!

3. Liam: I'm having a new computer game for my birthday.
   Kelly: Are you? I'd like to try it.

4. Charlie: Are you in the play? I'm going to be the dragon.
   Zoe: I don't know yet. I'd like to be the queen.

UNIT 10

# Pronouns

A **pronoun** is a word which **takes the place of a noun.**

Kate lost the needle. **She** (Kate) could not find **it** (the needle) anywhere.

These are **pronouns**. The **nouns** they replace are in brackets.

## Practice

**Here are some very common pronouns.**

| I | me | myself | you | yourself | yourselves | he | him | himself | she |
|---|---|---|---|---|---|---|---|---|---|
| her | herself | it | itself | we | us | ourselves | they | them | themselves |

**Copy the sentences. Complete them with pronouns from the box.**

1. I like these sweets. ______ are my favourites.
2. Ben put his book down. In the morning ______ could not find ______ anywhere.
3. When Gemma was undressed ______ got into the bath.
4. Mrs Smith ran after Sam and me. ______ chased ______ down the path.
5. The girl listened to her father because ______ thought ______ was right.
6. Don't climb the cliffs or you might hurt ______.
7. When the dog got wet ______ shook ______ all over Jake!
8. Peter washed ______ until ______ was completely clean.
9. The man gave a present to his wife. ______ wrapped ______ before ______ gave ______ to ______ .
10. We got top marks in the test. ______ were very pleased with ______ .

## Making sure

**The pronouns I and me are often confused.**
**If the word is part of the subject of a sentence, use I.**
**If it is part of the predicate of a sentence, use me.**
**Always put yourself last.**

**Rewrite these sentences, completing each one with I or me.**
**The first two have been done for you.**

1. Will and ___I___ are eating fish and chips.
2. The teacher gave the book to James and ___me___.
3. The dog belongs to Jason and _______.
4. My dad and _______ went to the cinema last night.
5. My cat and _______ both like milk.
6. Tom does not like Shannon and _______.
7. Gran spilled her drink over George and _______.
8. My friend and _______ went shopping.
9. Francis invited Richard and _______ to tea.
10. Uncle Bob and _______ enjoy playing football.

## Practise your punctuation

1. Punctuate these sentences correctly.
   a) get up mark or you will be late for school shouted mr bentall
   b) the bike has a puncture where can I get it mended
   c) emma likes crisps biscuits sweets and ice creams
      they are all bad for her
   d) last night dean and I went to see a film we liked it very much
   e) shall we catch the bus or the train mrs croft asked us
   f) help an alien has landed it is coming to get me

2. Now underline all the pronouns in the sentences you have written.

# Progress Test A

1. Copy these sentences. Write **n** above each **noun**, **v** above each **verb**, **adj** above each **adjective** and **adv** above each **adverb**.
   a) The brown dog barked loudly.
   b) Suddenly an enormous snake appeared.
   c) The noisy girls chatted excitedly.
   d) Quietly the burglar crept along the stone path.

2. Copy these sentences. After each, write **s** if it is a **statement**, **c** if it is a **command**, **q** if it is a **question** or **e** if it is an **exclamation**.
   a) How are you?
   b) Come here.
   c) I am going to school.
   d) I feel terrible!

3. Write the **past tense** of each verb. The first one has been done for you.
   a) catch → caught
   b) hug
   c) run
   d) live
   e) hold
   f) tell
   g) swim
   h) write
   i) walk
   j) cut

4. Copy and complete the chart.

| *Adjective* | *Comparative adjective* | *Superlative adjective* |
|---|---|---|
| bright | brighter | |
| pretty | | prettiest |
| helpful | | |
| anxious | | |
| heavy | | |
| bad | | |
| good | | |

5. Underline the **auxiliary verbs** in these sentences.
   a) The frog can jump very high.
   b) She must go to the shops.
   c) Ben has scored a goal.
   d) The spacecraft will reach Venus.

6. Copy the chart. Write each **adverb** from the box in the correct column.

| *Adverbs of manner* | *Adverbs of time* | *Adverbs of place* |
|---|---|---|
| | | |

| | | | | | |
|---|---|---|---|---|---|
| after | softly | there | loudly | down | next |
| now | wearily | lastly | here | inside | quickly |

7. Write the **plural** of each of these **nouns**.
   a) echo  b) thief  c) woman  d) child  e) potato  f) wife

8. Complete each phrase with a **plural noun** or a **collective noun**.
   a) a flock of ________
   b) a ________ of grapes
   c) an army of ________
   d) a ________ of fish
   e) a choir of ________
   f) a ________ of cows

9. Complete the sentences with suitable **pronouns**.
   a) I like baked beans. ________ are delicious.
   b) Ellen took her trainers off. ________ forgot to put ________ in her bag.
   c) When Edward got home ________ did his homework.
   d) Mr Bryant's dog was enormous but ________ was quite tame.

10. Complete each sentence with **I** or **me**.
   a) Lauren and ________ are going to school.
   b) Mrs McDonald gave Matthew and ________ a drink.
   c) My friend and ________ went to the park.
   d) Our neighbour likes my dog and ________.

# UNIT 11 Sentences (subject, verb and object)

Every **sentence** must have a **subject** and a **verb**.

Some **sentences** also have an **object**.

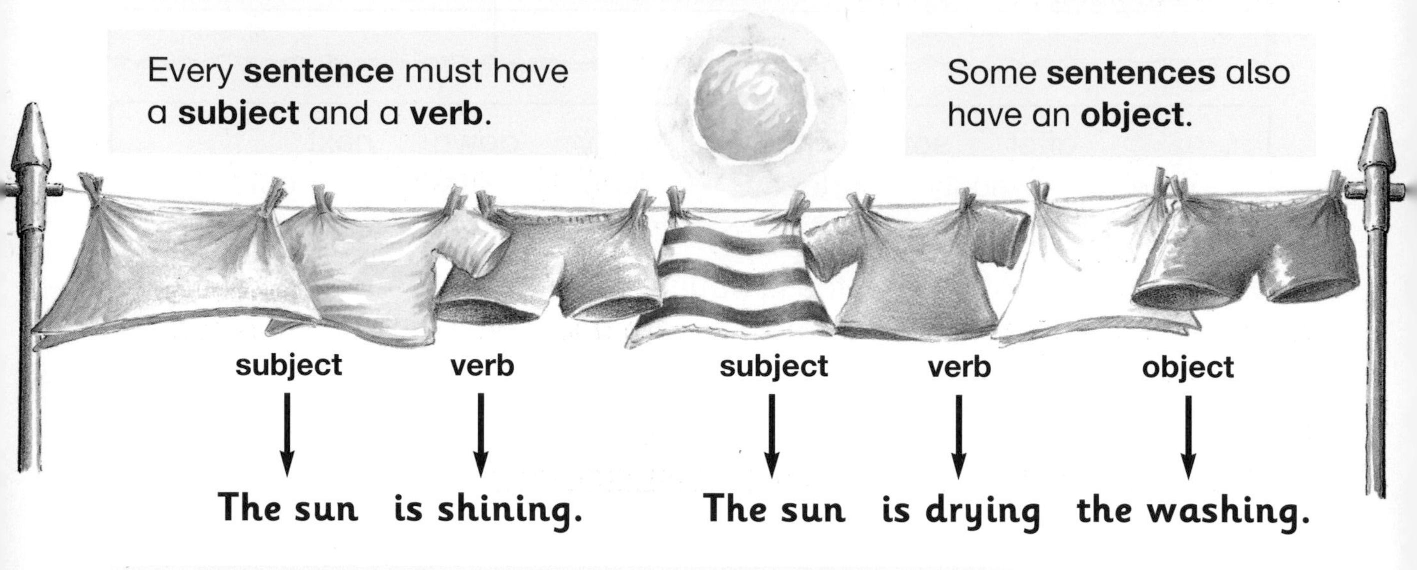


The **object** is the person or thing that is **affected by the verb**.
The **object** usually comes **after the verb** in a sentence.
**Not all verbs** can have an **object**.

## Practice

1. Choose a suitable object to complete each sentence.
   a) The hot sun melted ________.
   b) Tracey threw ________.
   c) The old man opened ________.
   d) I like eating ________.
   e) The beautiful princess kissed ________.
   f) My mum baked ________.
   g) Mrs Oliver dusted ________.
   h) The jockey mounted ________.
   i) Steffi won ________.
   j) Mr Roberts stirred ________.

2. Now underline and mark the subject, verb and object in each sentence. The first one has been done for you.

   s v o
   a) The hot sun melted the snow.

## Making sure

1. Rewrite these sentences. Change each pronoun into a suitable noun. The first one has been done for you.
   a) They like them. Darren and Rosie like mushroom omelettes.
   b) The teacher praised him.
   c) He caught the thieves.
   d) They hate it.
   e) It followed them.
   f) She found them.
   g) He patted it.
   h) We beat them.

2. Now underline and mark the subject, verb and object in each sentence. The first one has been done for you.

   a) Rosie and Darren (s) like (v) mushroom omelettes (o).

## Practise your punctuation

1. Make up six silly sentences using the subjects, verbs and objects in the boxes below. You can add any extra words you like. Punctuate your sentences correctly. One has been done for you.

*Subjects*
teacher monster queen alien crocodile doctor boys explorer astronaut lion magician man gardener prime minister

*Verbs*
scratched ate cooked met tickled chased hit kicked kissed cut swallowed broke grabbed shook

*Objects*
queen soldier cake elephant television crisps frog girls tummy football beard lorry dragon table

The enormous crocodile kissed the queen.

2. Now underline and mark the subject, verb and object in each sentence.

# UNIT 12 Possessive Nouns

A **possessive noun** tells us who the **owner** of something is.

my **mother's** cottage
(the cottage belonging to my mother)

We use an **apostrophe** to help make a **possessive noun**. This is an **apostrophe** ’
If there is just one owner we add **’s** to make the noun a **possessive noun**.

## Practice

**Rewrite these sentences. Include a possessive noun in each one. The first one has been done for you.**

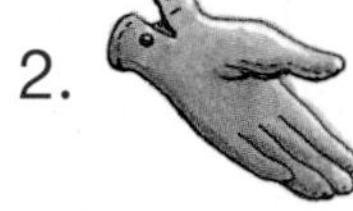

1.  The torch belongs to the burglar.
   It is the burglar's torch.

2.  The glove belongs to the woman.

3.  The car belongs to the robber.

4.  The pencils belong to the teacher.

5.  The shop belongs to Mr Patel.

6. 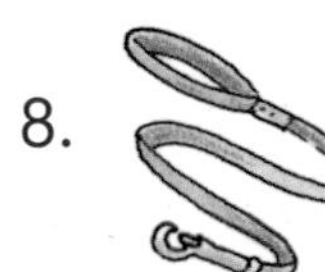 The bike belongs to Lisa.

7. The banana belongs to the gorilla.

8. The lead belongs to Fido.

9.  The trousers belong to Mark.

10.  The ring belongs to the queen.

## Making sure

1. When there is more than one owner, we add **’** to the plural noun to make it a possessive noun.

   the teachers’ car park

   When the plural noun does not end in **s**, we add **’s**.

   the children’s books

   Write these out in full. The first one has been done for you.
   a) It is the dragons’ cave. The cave belongs to the dragons.
   b) They are the men’s cars.
   c) They are the ladies’ skirts.
   d) They are the horses’ saddles.
   e) It is the girls’ bedroom.
   f) They are the churches’ doors.

2. Explain the difference between the possessive nouns.

| | |
|---|---|
| a) the teacher’s eyes | the teachers’ eyes |
| b) the footballer’s shorts | the footballers’ shorts |
| c) the hen’s eggs | the hens’ eggs |
| d) the bird’s wings | the birds’ wings |
| e) the fox’s cubs | the foxes’ cubs |

## Practise your punctuation

**Punctuate these sentences correctly.**

1. dr turners car was dirty rusty and badly repaired
2. mrs banks who was getting very angry shouted pass me sams trousers will you
3. his sisters name was alice
4. harrys house was near mr clarkes field
5. dont pull the crocodiles tail or itll bite you warned the zoo keeper
6. the babies clothes were hanging on the line

# UNIT 13 Possessive Adjectives and Possessive Pronouns

A **possessive adjective** tells us who the **owner** of something is.

A **possessive pronoun** tells us the same thing.

This is **my** tent.

This tent is **mine**.

**Possessive adjectives** and **possessive pronouns** do **not** take an apostrophe.

## Practice

1. Copy the sentences. Underline the possessive adjectives.

| my | your | his | her | its | our | their |
|---|---|---|---|---|---|---|

The first one has been done for you.

a) <u>Our</u> school is the best.
b) "Where is your friend?" my dad called.
c) Sara wore her new dress and William wore his new trainers.
d) The lost dog found its way home.
e) Indira and Karen looked for their shoes.

2. Rewrite these sentences. Replace each of the underlined words or groups of words with a possessive adjective. You may need to make some other changes as well.

a) Ben bought <u>Ben's</u> comic at the shop.
b) Emma spent all <u>Emma's</u> money on sweets.
c) Alan and Alice went off on <u>Alan's and Alice's</u> bikes.
d) The car <u>which belongs to us</u> is in the garage.
e) This is the telescope <u>which belongs to me</u>.

## Making sure

**Copy the sentences. Complete each one with a suitable possessive pronoun from the box.**

| mine | yours | his | hers | ours | theirs |
|---|---|---|---|---|---|

1. This cat belongs to me. It is ________.
2. That cat belongs to you. It is ________.
3. The green car belongs to him. It is ________.
4. You must take the responsibility. The responsibility is ________.
5. The red van belongs to them. It is ________.
6. The books on the table belong to Tim and me. They are ________.
7. Sally has taken the books that belong to her. They are ________.
8. I think the blue pencils belong to you. They must be ________.
9. I found the money so it is ________ now.
10. Do these slippers belong to you? Are they ________?

## Practise your punctuation

1. Copy this passage, punctuating it correctly.
   Don't forget to start a new line each time someone new speaks.

   on his way home from school tom found
   a bag on the ground is this yours he asked
   tara no its not my bag I left mine at
   school I think it might be emma's bag
   because hers is blue and green tom
   laughed and said you may be right
   she is always losing her things the
   two children picked up the bag
   and continued on their way

2. Underline all the possessive adjectives and possessive pronouns in the passage.
   a) Write **pa** above each possessive adjective.
   b) Write **pp** above each possessive pronoun.

UNIT 14

# Phrases

A **phrase** is a **group of words** which forms **part of a sentence.**
**Phrases** are usually quite **short**.
They **do not make sense** on their own.

I **staggered about** in **a slimy mud puddle**.

This is a **verb phrase.** It is based on the verb **staggered.**

This is a **noun phrase.** It is based on the noun **puddle.**

## Practice

1. Choose the most suitable noun phrase to completeeach sentence.

| the pirate ship | green smoke | an exciting cover |
|---|---|---|
| small, fluffy chicks | the best swimmer | |

a) The hen had several ___________.
b) ___________ sank in the storm.
c) The history book had ___________.
d) Patrick is ___________ in our class.
e) The fearful dragon breathed ___________ from its nostrils.

2. Choose the most suitable verb phrase to complete each sentence.

| couldn't find | was still wrapping | came rushing |
|---|---|---|
| would have loved | can be made | |

a) Several small children ___________ towards us.
b) Father Christmas ___________ the presents on Christmas Eve.
c) Statues ___________ from wood or stone.
d) Tom ___________ his puppy in the woods.
e) Uncle John ___________ to go up in a hot air balloon.

## Making sure

1. Copy the sentences. Complete each one with a suitable noun phrase.
   a) The old car chugged slowly up ___________.
   b) ___________ charged bravely into battle.
   c) In my bag I found ___________.
   d) The best thing ever invented is ___________.
   e) ___________ threw jelly all over the place.

2. Copy the sentences. Complete each one with a suitable verb phrase.
   a) Gina ___________ at ten o'clock on Thursday.
   b) The beautiful picture ___________ in lovely colours.
   c) I don't think John ___________ after all.
   d) If you make a cake you ___________ eggs and flour.
   e) The angry man ___________ out of the front door.

## Practise your punctuation

1. Punctuate these sentences correctly.
   a) a being from the planet astra landed in a spaceship
   b) in december the people of scotland were terrified by a dragon
   c) come quickly Ive found a box jim shouted excitedly
   d) the man called out in a loud voice stop dont move
   e) mrs birch baked a cake but billys dog ate it
   f) a strong wind blew through the trees

2. Now rewrite the sentences. Make them more interesting by using noun phrases in place of some of the nouns. The first one has been done for you.

   a) A weird, four-eyed, smoke-breathing being from the Planet Astra landed in a huge, silver spaceship.

UNIT

# 15 Paragraphs

A **paragraph** is a **group of sentences** that deals with **one main idea** or topic. A long piece of writing is **easier to read** if it is divided into **paragraphs**.

We begin a new **paragraph** by starting the first line a little way in from the margin. (This is called **indenting**.)

→ A waterfall is a stream of water which descends suddenly to a lower level. If the volume of water is small, it is called a cascade; if large, it is called a cataract.

→ Angel Falls, in the Guiana Highlands of Venezuela, are the world's largest falls, with the longest uninterrupted drop. They were discovered in 1935 by an American aviator, James Angel.

→ Niagara Falls are among the most famous falls in the world. They are located on the Niagara River, about 16 miles north-west of Buffalo, New York. Niagara Falls consist of two cataracts: the Horseshoe (or Canadian) Falls and the American Falls. The international boundary line between Canada and the United States passes through the centre of the Horseshoe Falls.

## Practice

1. The first paragraph tells us what a waterfall is.
   a) What is the second paragraph about?
   b) What is the third paragraph about?

2. Write a paragraph about each of the following:
   a) My family
   b) My friends
   c) My relatives

## Making sure

1. Write a short paragraph about each picture.
   Give your story a suitable title.

2. Write two paragraphs.
   In the first paragraph, put forward some arguments in favour of school uniform.
   In the second paragraph, put forward some arguments against it.

3. Here is the opening paragraph of a story. Write two more paragraphs to continue the story.

   It started off as an ordinary day. Then the letter dropped through the letter box. There was no stamp on it and it was addressed in the strangest handwriting. When I opened it, I was amazed!

## Practise your punctuation

**Rewrite this passage in three paragraphs.**
**Punctuate the passage correctly.**

lakes result from the flow of water into low areas lake water comes largely from rainfall and melting snow the water enters a lake basin through brooks streams rivers and underground springs sometimes a lake is formed when the crater of an extinct volcano fills with water crater lake in oregon is an example of this lakes may also be artificially made when a dam is built across a river valley it will block the flow of water and form a lake lake mead was formed when the hoover dam was built on the colorado river

UNIT 16

# Sentences
## (subject and verb agreement)

Every **sentence** must have a **subject** and a **verb**. The **verb** must always **agree with** (match) the **subject**.

s v
**The captain was** worried.

When the **subject** is **singular** we must use the **singular** form of the **verb** with it.

s v
**They were** a great distance from the shore.

When the **subject** is **plural** we must use the **plural** form of the **verb** with it.

## Practice

1. Choose a suitable singular noun to go with the verb in each of these sentences.
   a) A twig floats. b) ________ flies. c) ________ jumps.
   d) ________ sinks. e) ________ hops. f) ________ crawls.

2. Choose a suitable plural noun to go with the verb in each of these sentences.
   a) Twigs float. b) ________ fly. c) ________ jump.
   d) ________ sink. e) ________ hop. f) ________ crawl.

3. Choose the correct form of the verb to complete each sentence.
   a) Auntie Jane (like/likes) ice cream.
   b) The settee (need/needs) some soft cushions.
   c) The children (wear/wears) jeans.
   d) The detective (solve/solves) the mystery.
   e) Doctors (check/checks) us to make sure we are healthy.
   f) The telephone (ring/rings) loudly.
   g) Sharks (live/lives) in the sea.

4. Underline all the subjects and all the verbs in the sentences you have written for Question 3.
   a) Write **s** above each subject.
   b) Write **v** above each verb.

## Making sure

1. Copy and complete this chart.

| | Verbs | | | | | |
|---|---|---|---|---|---|---|
| | *to be* (present tense) | *to be* (past tense) | *to do* (present tense) | *to do* (past tense) | *to have* (present tense) | *to have* (past tense) |
| *I* | am | | | did | have | |
| *you* | are | | | | | had |
| *he* | is | | does | | | |
| *she* | | | | | has | |
| *it* | | was | | | | had |
| *we* | | were | | did | | |
| *you* | | | do | | have | |
| *they* | are | | do | | have | |

2. Choose the correct form of the verb to complete each sentence.
   a) Art (is/are) my favourite subject.
   b) The rowdy children (was/were) making a lot of noise.
   c) (Was/were) you late for school this morning?
   d) They (wasn't/weren't) very good apples.
   e) I (done/did) it.
   f) Tom (have/has) a lot of work to do.

## Practise your punctuation

1. Punctuate these sentences correctly.
   a) where is the car going
   b) a fox lives in a home called a den
   c) the boy does well at spelling reading maths and science
   d) in the morning the bus arrives here
   e) the small girl who has a dirty face enjoys chocolate
   f) the frog which is large and fat hops on to a rock
   g) hasn't the footballer scored yet

2. Now rewrite the sentences. Change the subject and verb in each into the plural form. You may need to make some other changes as well.

UNIT 17

# Prepositions

A **preposition** is a word that tells us the **position** of one thing **in relation to another**.

The train goes **through** the tunnel.

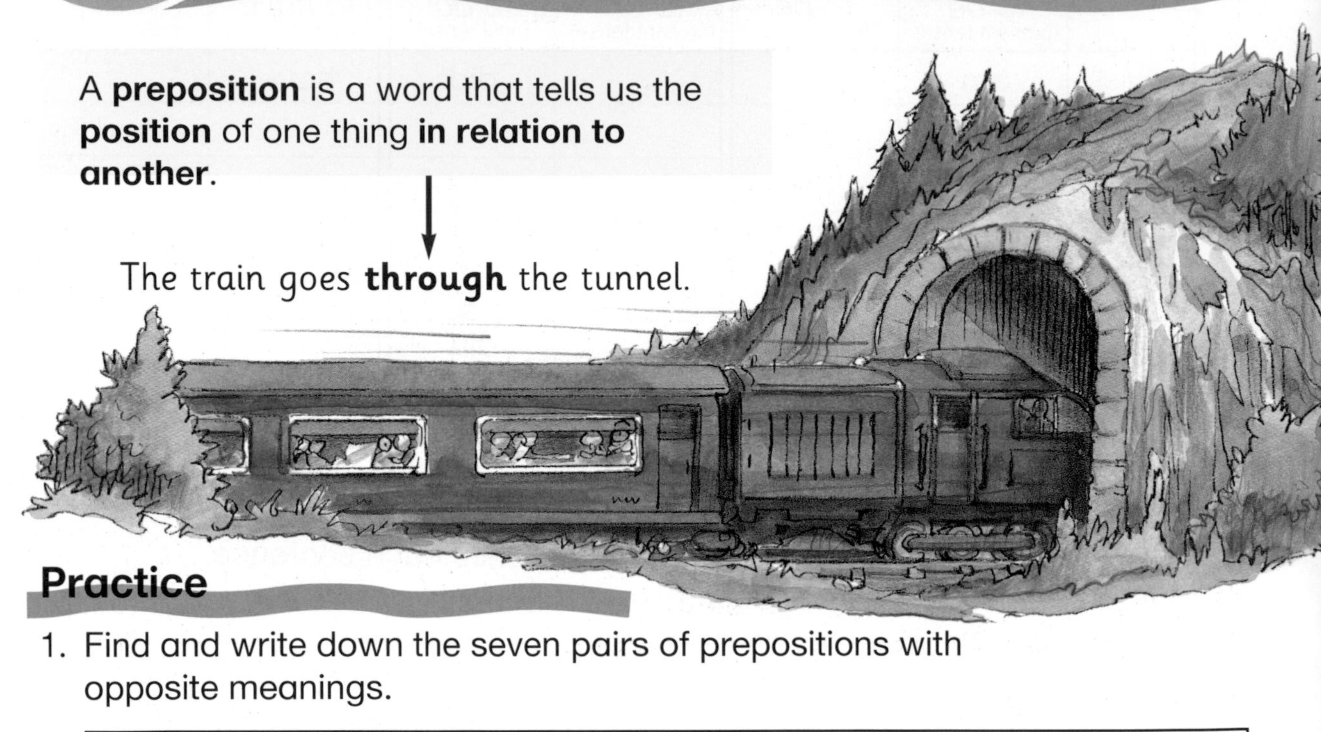

## Practice

1. Find and write down the seven pairs of prepositions with opposite meanings.

| *Set A* | | | | | | |
|---|---|---|---|---|---|---|
| on | above | over | down | inside | with | from |

| *Set B* | | | | | | |
|---|---|---|---|---|---|---|
| up | off | to | without | below | outside | under |

2. Find and circle the preposition hidden in each of these words.
   a) rounder b) supply c) rain
   d) coffee e) hovered f) spoon g) pastry

3. Complete each sentence with a suitable preposition.
   a) The dog jumped __________ the wall.
   b) A grey squirrel climbed __________ the oak tree.
   c) Emma wrote __________ her penfriend.
   d) The seal dived __________ the cold sea.
   e) A police helicopter flew __________ the trees.
   f) I found my lost sock __________ the bed.
   g) The train pulled __________ the station.

## Making sure

**Complete each sentence with a preposition from the box. The first one has been done for you.**

| with | from | against | of | to | for | on |
|---|---|---|---|---|---|---|

1. The shop was full ___of___ people.
2. Don't rely ________ me.
3. I agreed ________ the politician.
4. My coat is similar ________ yours.
5. I was ashamed ________ myself.
6. The boy protested ________ his punishment.
7. Apples are good ________ you.
8. Don't be angry ________ me.
9. Stuart was suffering ________ a bad cold.
10. I was guilty ________ telling a lie.
11. My shirt is different ________ yours.
12. Please wait ________ me.

## Practise your punctuation

1. Punctuate this passage correctly.

   did you know that mountain gorillas are found in africa they live in groups in the high mountain ranges as they move through the forests they search for fruit and roots their movement depends upon the weather but as a general rule they may travel between two and three miles a day gorillas live on the ground but the younger ones climb trees after fruit sometimes throwing some of it down to the older members of the group

2. Now find and underline the prepositions in the passage.

UNIT 18

# Clauses

A **clause** is a **group of words** which can be used either as a **whole sentence** or as **part of a sentence**.
A **clause** must always contain a **verb**.

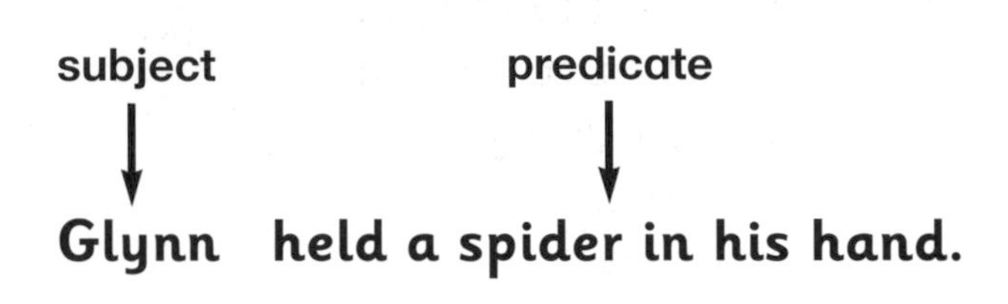


A simple **one-clause sentence** is always made up of two parts:
- a **subject** (who or what the sentence is about)
- a **predicate** (the rest of the sentence)

## Practice

1. Find a suitable subject to go with each predicate.
   a) _________ ate a huge apple pie.
   b) _________ counted up the money in the till.
   c) _________ won the cup.
   d) _________ travel underwater.

2. Find a suitable predicate to go with each subject.
   a) The Loch Ness Monster _________.
   b) My family _________.
   c) It _________.
   d) Seven sheep, ten hens, two horses and a goat _________.

3. Copy these one-clause sentences. Divide each one into subject and predicate. Underline the verb in each predicate.
   The first one has been done for you.
   a) My best friend <u>came</u> to tea.
   b) Curry tastes very spicy.
   c) Our teacher shouted at us.
   d) We cycled all the way home.

## Making sure

1. We can make a two-clause sentence by joining two short sentences with a **conjunction** (a connective). Make each pair of short sentences into a longer, two-clause sentence by joining them with the conjunction **and** or the conjunction **but**. The first one has been done for you.

   a) The girls fetched their bikes. They went to the park.
      The girls fetched their bikes and went to the park.
   b) The spider had eight legs. It crawled slowly.
   c) I love cauliflower. I do not like sprouts.
   d) We set out early. We had a good time.
   e) I enjoy watching television. Our television is broken.
   f) We chose a pizza. We ordered it from the waiter.
   g) Tom scored full marks in spelling. He only got one sum correct.
   h) The workman mixed the cement. He tipped it into the hole.

2. Now underline the two clauses in each sentence you have written. The first one has been done for you.

   a) The girls fetched their bikes and went to the park.

## Practise your punctuation

1. Punctuate these sentences correctly. Underline the conjunction in each one.
   a) the lady went into the shop and bought a new dress
   b) tara shut the door but left the window open
   c) we saw manchester united play when we were visiting uncle paul
   d) there were eight of us so we had to take two cars
   e) the alsatian looked fierce but he was really quite tame
   f) tibs my cat is very fat and eats too much

2. Now rewrite each long sentence as two shorter, one-clause sentences. The first one has been done for you.

   a) The lady went into the shop. She bought a new dress.

UNIT 19

# Indirect Speech

We can write speech in two ways – as **direct speech** or as **indirect speech**.

**The jockey said, "My horse can gallop fast."**

This is written in **direct speech**. The jockey's exact words are enclosed in **inverted commas**.

**The jockey said that his horse could gallop fast.**

This is written in **indirect speech**. The jockey's exact words are **not** used, so **inverted commas** are **not needed**.

## Practice

**Change these sentences into indirect speech. You may have to change the words slightly. The first one has been done for you.**

1. "How old are you?" Carl asked the old lady.
   Carl asked the old lady how old she was.
2. The doctor said, "Please sit down, Mrs Williams."
3. "Help!" shouted the drowning man. "Throw me a lifebelt!"
4. "Take this book back to the shelves," the librarian said to Eve.
5. "Has anyone seen my crown?" the king asked.
6. The teacher looked at me and said, "You must learn your spellings."
7. "Mark," said his mother, "please get me some eggs from the shop."
8. "It's raining very heavily,"remarked Uncle John.
9. "These pills will soon make you better, Jane," said Dr Fisher.
10. The mechanic explained, "The brakes need mending, Mr Jones."

## Making sure

**Change these sentences into direct speech. The first one has been done for you.**

1. Mr Bertoli asked Marissa if she had hurt herself.
   "Have you hurt yourself, Marissa?"
   Mr Bertoli asked the girl.
2. The boy said that he knew the answer.
3. Mrs Azadi cried that she had lost her ring.
4. The old man remarked that he would be eighty next year.
5. Kerry told Gemma that she had just found some money.
6. Ruth's teacher asked her why she had been away last week.
7. The police officer reported that the house had been burgled.
8. The mountaineer boasted that he could easily climb the mountain.
9. The criminal protested that he was not guilty.
10. Sara's dad exclaimed that he would not buy her any new trainers.

## Practise your punctuation

1. Punctuate this short playscript correctly. (In playscripts you do not need to use inverted commas.) The first line has been done for you.

   mr parish: whats for tea tonight
   Mr Parish: What's for tea tonight?
   mrs parish: would you like curry spaghetti pizza or fish fingers
   mr parish: I think Id like hamburgers please
   mrs parish: just a minute I didnt offer you hamburgers
   mr parish: I know but theyre what I really fancy
   mrs parish: oh well youll just have to cook them yourself

2. Now rewrite this conversation using only indirect speech. Start it like this:

   Mr Parish asked his wife what was for tea that night.

# Verb Tenses (future)

This morning I **flew** over the mountains.

This happened in the **past**. The **verb** is in the **past tense**.

Now I **am flying** over the sea.

This is happening **now**. The **verb** is in the **present tense**.

This evening I **will fly** over my village.

This will happen in the **future**. The **verb** is in the **future tense**.

When we write verbs in the future tense we often use the auxiliary verb **will** to help the main verb.

## Practice

1. Put each of these sentences into the future tense. The first one has been done for you.

| *Present tense* | *Future tense* |
|---|---|
| a) Today I am riding a bike. | Tomorrow I will ride a bike. |
| b) Today you are digging the garden. | |
| c) Today he is doing maths. | |
| d) Today she is going to school. | |

2. Put each of these sentences into the past tense. The first one has been done for you.

| *Future tense* | *Past tense* |
|---|---|
| a) Tomorrow she will come. | Yesterday she came. |
| b) Tomorrow it will appear. | |
| c) Tomorrow we will dance. | |
| d) Tomorrow they will play. | |

## Making sure

1. Copy and complete this chart.

| *Present tense* | *Past tense* | *Future tense* |
|---|---|---|
| a) I sing | I sang | I will sing |
| b) You eat | You ate | |
| c) He washes | | |
| d) She likes | | |
| e) It disappears | | |
| f) We explain | | |
| g) I argue | | |
| h) You try | | |
| i) We grow | | |

2. Put all the verbs in this passage into the future tense. Start it like this:

   I will get up at seven o'clock

   I got up at seven o'clock and had my breakfast. I played football for half an hour and read my comic, and then I called for my friend. We walked to school and played in the playground. In the morning we had Maths and English. At lunchtime I had a jacket potato with cheese.

## Practise your punctuation

1. Punctuate this passage correctly.

   on wednesday sujata will run home from school and have a quick snack she will get changed and go into town with her mum mrs patel they will look for a present for her sister saimas birthday after this they will stay in town and choose sujata a new skirt jumper coat and pair of shoes what a busy evening it will be

2. Now rewrite the passage in the past tense. Start it like this:

   On Wednesday Sujata ran home from school and had a quick snack.

# Progress Test B

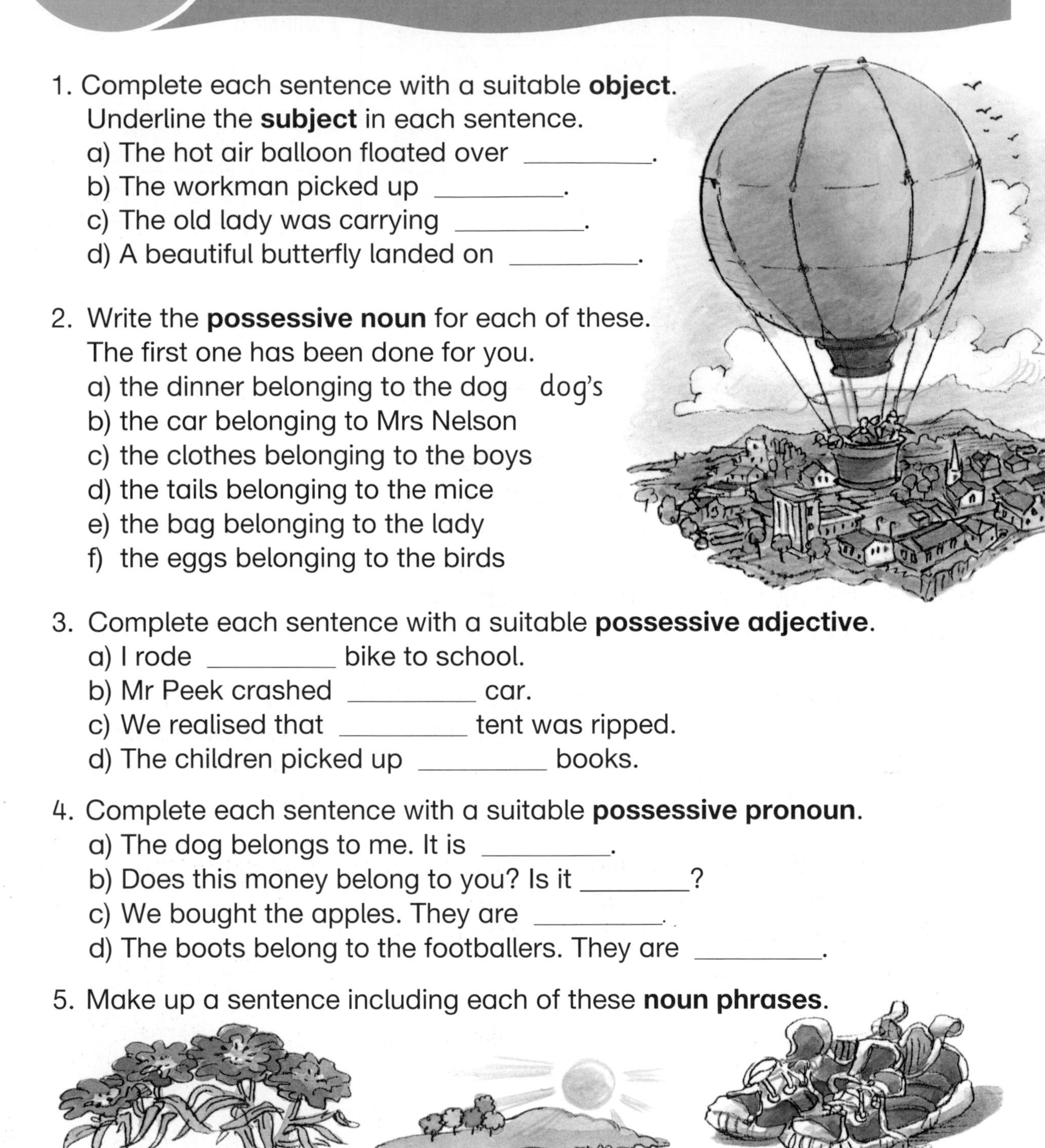

1. Complete each sentence with a suitable **object**. Underline the **subject** in each sentence.
   a) The hot air balloon floated over _________.
   b) The workman picked up _________.
   c) The old lady was carrying _________.
   d) A beautiful butterfly landed on _________.

2. Write the **possessive noun** for each of these. The first one has been done for you.
   a) the dinner belonging to the dog   dog's
   b) the car belonging to Mrs Nelson
   c) the clothes belonging to the boys
   d) the tails belonging to the mice
   e) the bag belonging to the lady
   f) the eggs belonging to the birds

3. Complete each sentence with a suitable **possessive adjective**.
   a) I rode _________ bike to school.
   b) Mr Peek crashed _________ car.
   c) We realised that _________ tent was ripped.
   d) The children picked up _________ books.

4. Complete each sentence with a suitable **possessive pronoun**.
   a) The dog belongs to me. It is _________.
   b) Does this money belong to you? Is it _________?
   c) We bought the apples. They are _________.
   d) The boots belong to the footballers. They are _________.

5. Make up a sentence including each of these **noun phrases**.

a) some purple flowers

b) a sunny afternoon

c) an old pair of trainers

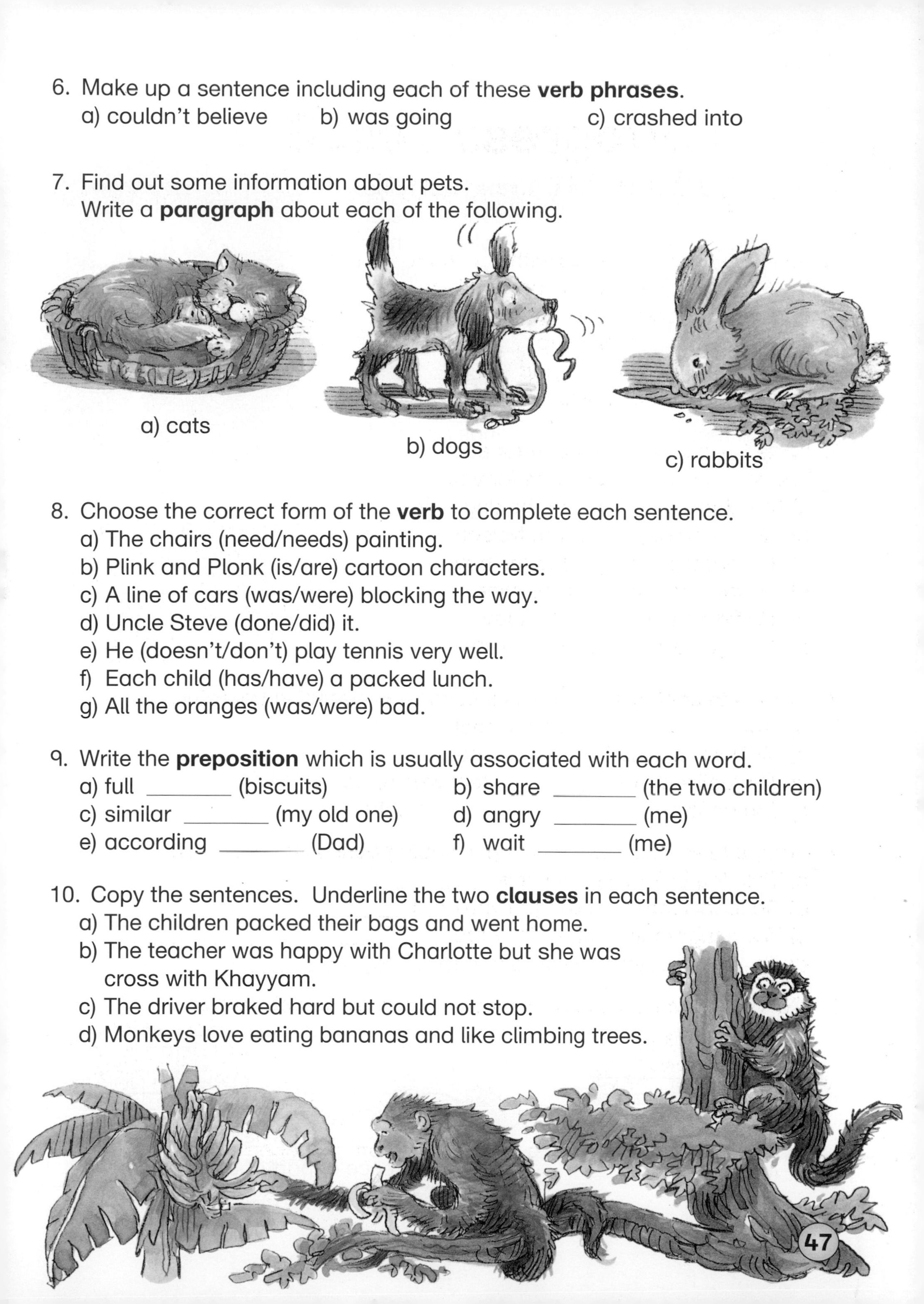

6. Make up a sentence including each of these **verb phrases**.
   a) couldn't believe  b) was going  c) crashed into

7. Find out some information about pets.
   Write a **paragraph** about each of the following.

   a) cats  b) dogs  c) rabbits

8. Choose the correct form of the **verb** to complete each sentence.
   a) The chairs (need/needs) painting.
   b) Plink and Plonk (is/are) cartoon characters.
   c) A line of cars (was/were) blocking the way.
   d) Uncle Steve (done/did) it.
   e) He (doesn't/don't) play tennis very well.
   f) Each child (has/have) a packed lunch.
   g) All the oranges (was/were) bad.

9. Write the **preposition** which is usually associated with each word.
   a) full ________ (biscuits)  b) share ________ (the two children)
   c) similar ________ (my old one)  d) angry ________ (me)
   e) according ________ (Dad)  f) wait ________ (me)

10. Copy the sentences. Underline the two **clauses** in each sentence.
    a) The children packed their bags and went home.
    b) The teacher was happy with Charlotte but she was cross with Khayyam.
    c) The driver braked hard but could not stop.
    d) Monkeys love eating bananas and like climbing trees.

11. Rewrite this passage. Put all the verbs into the **future tense**.

The pirate rowed his boat to the island and jumped on to the sand. He unloaded the box of jewels and looked for somewhere to hide it. He searched the whole island. The pirate found a good spot in a cave and buried the treasure there.

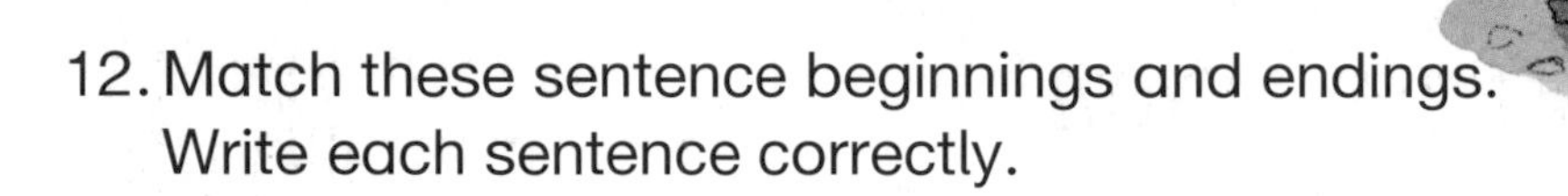

12. Match these sentence beginnings and endings. Write each sentence correctly.

| |  |  |
|---|---|---|
| a) | The object of a sentence | describes who something belongs to. |
| b) | A possessive noun | is a group of sentences that deal with one main idea. |
| c) | A possessive adjective | tells of something that will happen in the future. |
| d) | A phrase | is the person or thing affected by the verb. |
| e) | A paragraph | must always agree with the verb. |
| f) | The subject of a sentence | is a group of words which forms part of a sentence. |
| g) | A clause | always has an apostrophe in it. |
| h) | The future tense | is a group of words which contains a verb; it can be used as a complete sentence or part of a sentence. |